Guide

Washington

By Carole Marsh

The GALLOPADE GANG

Carole Marsh	Kathy Zimmer	Cranston Davenport
Bob Longmeyer	Terry Briggs	Lisa Stanley
Chad Beard	Pat Newman	Antoinette Miller
Cecil Anderson	Billie Walburn	Victoria DeJoy
Steven Saint-Laurent	Jackie Clayton	Al Fortunatti
Jill Sanders	Pam Dufresne	Shery Kearney

Published by GALLOPADE INTERNATIONAL

www.washingtonexperience.com
800-536-2GET • www.gallopade.com

©2001 Carole Marsh • First Edition • All Rights Reserved.
Character Illustrations by Lucyna A. M. Green.
No part of this publication may be reproduced in whole or in part, stored in a retrieval system, or transmitted in any form or by any means, electronic, mechanical, photocopying, recording or otherwise, without written permission from the publisher.

The Washington Experience logo is a trademark of Carole Marsh and Gallopade International, Inc. A free catalog of The Washington Experience Products is available by calling 800-536-2GET, or by visiting our website at www.washingtonexperience.com.

Gallopade is proud to be a member of these educational organizations and associations:

Other Washington Experience Products

- The Washington Experience!
- The BIG Washington Reproducible Activity Book
- The Washington Coloring Book
- My First Book About Washington!
- Washington "Jography": A Fun Run Through Our State
- Washington Jeopardy!: Answers and Questions About Our State
- The Washington Experience! Sticker Pack
- The Washington Experience! Poster/Map
- Discover Washington CD-ROM
- Washington "Geo" Bingo Game
- Washington "Histo" Bingo Game

A Word From the Author... (okay, a few words)...

Hi!

Here's your own handy pocket guide about the great state of Washington! It really will fit in a pocket—I tested it. And it really will be useful when you want to know a fact you forgot, to bone up for a test, or when your teacher says, "I wonder . . ." and you have the answer—instantly! Wow, I'm impressed!

Get smart, have fun!
Carole Marsh

Washington Basics explores your state's symbols and their special meanings!

Washington Geography digs up the what's where in your state!

Washington History is like traveling through time to some of your state's great moments!

Washington People introduces you to famous personalities and your next-door neighbors!

Washington Places shows you where you might enjoy your next family vacation!

Washington Nature - no preservatives here, just what Mother Nature gave to Washington!

All the real fun stuff that we just HAD to save for its own section!

- Washington Basics
- Washington Geography
- Washington History
- Washington People
- Washington Places
- Washington Nature
- Washington Miscellany

State Name

Who Named You?

Washington's official state name is...

Washington

State Name

Word Definition

OFFICIAL: appointed, authorized, or approved by a government or organization

Statehood: November 11, 1889

Washington was the 42nd state to join the Union.

Washington will be on a state-commemorative quarter starting in the year 2007. Look for it in cash registers everywhere!

Coccinella noemnotata is my name (that's Latin for ladybug)! What's YOURS?

State Name Origin

A Name of Presidential Proportions!

State Name Origin

When Washington became a territory in 1853, it was supposed to be named Columbia. However, members of Congress in Washington, D.C., changed the name to Washington to honor our first president—George Washington.

Washington is the only state named after a president!

Many of Washington's city names, such as Yakima and Walla Walla, reflect its Native American heritage.

State Nicknames

WHO Are You Calling Names?

State Nicknames

Washington is not the only name by which the state is recognized. Like many other states, Washington has some nicknames, official or unofficial!

The Evergreen State

Seattle pioneer and historian C.T. Conover gave Washington its nickname because of its abundant evergreen forests. The state legislature adopted the nickname in 1893.

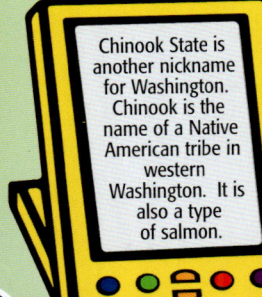

Chinook State is another nickname for Washington. Chinook is the name of a Native American tribe in western Washington. It is also a type of salmon.

State Capital/Capitol

State Capital: Olympia

Since 1853

State Capital/ Capitol

In 1845, Olympia was settled as the village of Smithfield, which was a shipping port for logging firms. Congress renamed the village Olympia after it was named a port of entry in 1851. When Washington became a territory in 1853, Olympia was named as capital. Olympia is located on the southern end of Puget Sound, on Budd Inlet at the mouth of the Deschutes River.

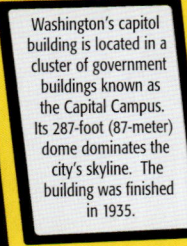

Washington's capitol building is located in a cluster of government buildings known as the Capital Campus. Its 287-foot (87-meter) dome dominates the city's skyline. The building was finished in 1935.

Word Definition

CAPITAL: a town or city that is the official seat of government
CAPITOL: the building in which the government officials meet

State Government

Who's in Charge Here?

Washington's GOVERNMENT has three branches:

- **LEGISLATIVE**
- **EXECUTIVE**
- **JUDICIAL**

State Government

- **Legislative:** Two Houses: The Senate (49 members) House of Representatives (98 members)
- **Executive:** A governor, lieutenant governor, secretary of state, attorney general, and other elected officials
- **Judicial:** Supreme Court has nine justices. Lesser courts include court of appeals, district superior courts, and justice-of-the-peace courts.

The number of legislators is determined by population, which is counted in the census every ten years. The numbers above are certain to change as Washington grows and prospers.

When you are 18 and register according to Washington laws, you can vote! So please do! Your vote counts!

State Flag

State Flag

Washington's current state flag was adopted in 1923. It features the state seal centered on a dark green field.

As you travel throughout Washington, count the times you see the Washington flag! Look for it on government vehicles, too!

State Seal & Motto

State Seal

The Talcott brothers designed the state seal. Charles used an ink bottle, silver dollar, and a postage stamp with George Washington's picture on it. L. Grant added the words, "The Seal of the State of Washington, 1889." Washington became a state in 1889. Another Talcott brother, G.N., cut the printing die, the tool used to make the seal.

MOTTO: a sentence, phrase, or word expressing the spirit or purpose of an organization or group

State Motto

Washington's state motto is...

Al-ki or Alki.

It is an Indian word meaning "bye and bye" or "hope for the future."

A design committee asked Olympia jeweler Charles Talcott to create a seal before the first meeting of the state legislature in 1889. After looking at a more detailed design, Charles came up with the simple, timeless seal.

You can find the state seal on government papers

State Bird

Birds of a Feather

Willow goldfinches are small and live in fields and meadows, or small trees. Male willow goldfinches have bright yellow feathers, a black forehead, black wings and a black tail with white edges. The females are a dull yellow-brown with black wings, and no black forehead. Willow goldfinches like to eat weed seeds, grain, and wild fruit.

State Bird

The willow goldfinch is often called the "wild canary."

Is this a picture of the male or female willow goldfinch?

ANSWER: the male

State Tree

WESTERN HEMLOCK

State Tree

Woodman, spare that tree! —George Pope Morris

The western hemlock became the state tree in 1947. It grows to more than 200 feet (60.9 meters) tall. The timber from the western hemlock is used for construction, boxing, and pulpwood. Hemlocks have short, flat needles on small stalks, in two flattened rows.

State Flower

Coast Rhododendron

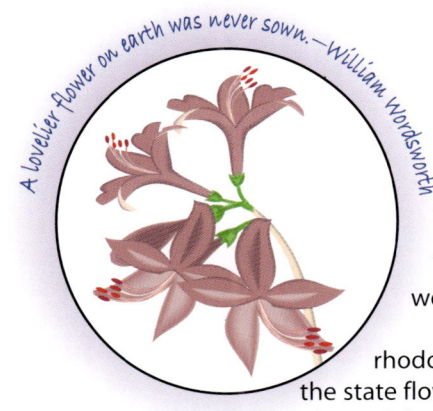

A lovelier flower on earth was never sown. —William Wordsworth

State Flower

Washington women chose the coast rhododendron as the state flower in 1892. An official flower was needed to exhibit at the 1893 World's Fair in Chicago. Women across the state voted on two finalists, the clover and rhododendron. The rhododendron received 53 percent of the votes. Rhododendrons' leaves are evergreen, and the flowers are pink, white, yellow, red, and purple.

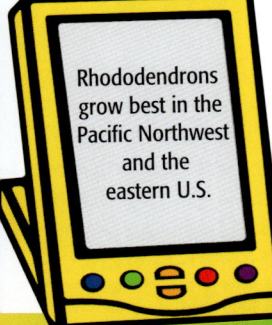

Rhododendrons grow best in the Pacific Northwest and the eastern U.S.

RIDDLE:
If the state flower got mixed up with the state gem, what would you have?

ANSWER: A bunch of sticks—it could happen!

State Tartan

State Tartan

Washington designated a state tartan in 1991. It was designed in 1988 by Margaret McLeod van Nus and Frank Cannonita of the Vancouver, USA Country Dancers for the Washington State Centennial (100th) celebration. The tartan has a green background which represents the state's rich forests. The bands of contrasting colors, and what they represent, are blue for rivers, lakes, and the ocean; white for snow-capped mountains; red for apples and cherries; yellow for wheat and grain crops; and black for the eruption of Mount St. Helen's.

A tartan is a design for weaving cloth in a plaid pattern with contrasting colors on a solid background.

Tartan is the traditional dress of the Scottish Highlands. The association between Scottish clans (a group of families with a common ancestor) and a particular pattern of tartan started in the 19th century.

State Gem and Fossil

PETRIFIED WOOD

Layers of logs were preserved by lava flows from Washington's volcanoes. The logs became like stone (petrified) after hot, silica-filled water seeped in and covered them. Petrified wood looks just like it did thousands of years ago!

State Gem and Fossil

COLUMBIAN MAMMOTH

Nearly all mammoths died out 10,000 years ago. Columbian mammoth fossils have been found on the Olympic Peninsula. The mammoths liked to eat grass. The males grew to the size of modern elephants. Females were about half the size of males. The mammoths used their tusks for protection and for digging food in the snow.

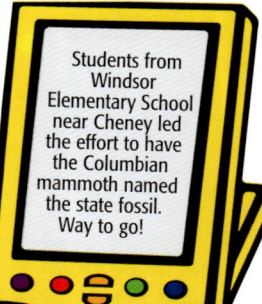

Students from Windsor Elementary School near Cheney led the effort to have the Columbian mammoth named the state fossil. Way to go!

State Dance

SQUARE DANCE

State Dance

Pioneers brought a dance called the *quadrille*, which means square in French, with them when they came west to Washington. The pioneers liked the term "square" better than "*quadrille*," so they called the dance the square dance. In a square dance, an even number of couples arrange themselves facing each other in either a straight line or a circle. A caller directs the dancers in which steps to perform. Square dances are known for their figures and footwork.

The square dance became Washington's official state dance on April 17, 1979.

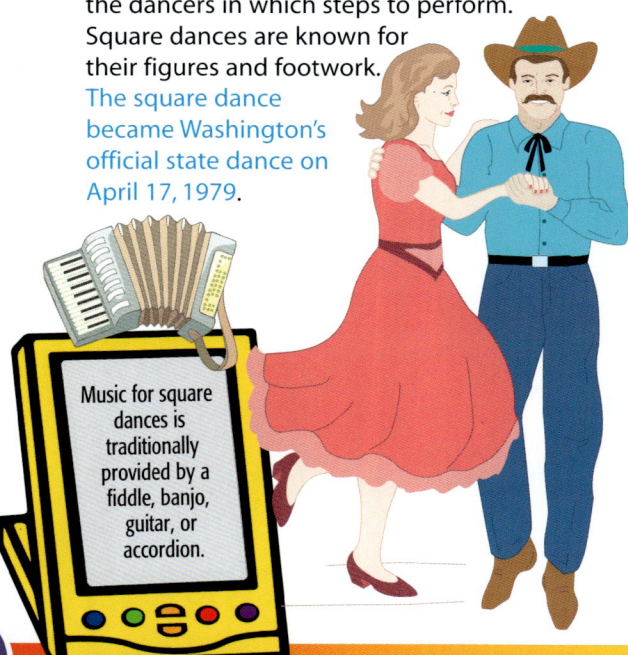

Music for square dances is traditionally provided by a fiddle, banjo, guitar, or accordion.

State Fruit

APPLE

State Fruit

Washington is the top apple-producing state in the U.S.! In 1989, the state's 100th anniversary, the apple was named the state fruit. Washington apples come in many colors, sizes, and varieties. Most of the 172,000 acres (69,608 hectares) of apple orchards in the state are located in eastern Washington.

An apple a day keeps the doctor away!

More than half the fresh apples grown in the U.S. are grown in Washington.

State Songs

"Washington, My Home"

Adopted as the state song in 1959, "Washington, My Home" was written by Helen Davis and arranged by Stuart Churchill.

This is my country; God gave it to me;
I will protect it. Ever keep it free.
Small towns and cities rest here in the sun,
filled with our laughter, thy will be done.

(refrain)
Washington is my home; Where ever I may roam:
This is my land, my native land, Washington, my home.

Our verdant forest green, Caressed by silv'ry stream,
From mountain peak to fields of wheat, Washington, my home.
There's peace you feel and understand. In this, our own beloved land.
We greet the day with head held high, and forward ever is our cry.
We'll happy ever be as people always free.

For you and me a destiny; Washington my home.
For you and me a destiny; Washington my home.

The state folk song is "Roll On, Columbia, Roll On" by Woody Guthrie.

VERDANT: lush, green growth

Word Definition

State Insect & Grass

Green Darner Dragonfly

The green darner dragonfly was adopted as state insect in 1997. It is found throughout Washington and eats a lot of insect pests. It has a bright green head and thorax (chest) and can fly 25–35 miles (40–56 kilometers) per hour.

State Insect & Grass

Bluebunch Wheatgrass

Bluebunch wheatgrass grows in eastern Washington. It was the main food for livestock in Washington's early history. It still is an important source of food for cattle, deer, elk, and other wildlife. Bluebunch wheatgrass can be seen along the Snake and Columbia rivers and in eastern Washington state parks.

The green darner dragonfly is also known as the "mosquito hawk." There are over 400 different species of dragonflies.

A dragonfly's wings are always outspread, whether resting or flying!

State Fish

Steelhead Trout

Steelhead trout is one of Washington's most popular fish for recreational fishing. It was adopted as state fish in 1969. It is anadromous, which means it returns to fresh water from the salt water to spawn (lay eggs). A steelhead's scales shine with flecks of silver. It has a gray spotted back and a white belly,

State Fish

TASTY TROUT

Put a trout filet on foil. Drizzle with lemon juice. Sprinkle with salt and pepper. Add shredded smoked ham and broil fish until done.

Sounds fishy to me!

State Map

The State of
Washington

State Map

Washington state is rectangular in shape, with a "bite" taken out of the northwest corner at the Pacific Ocean.

Munch, munch!

State Location

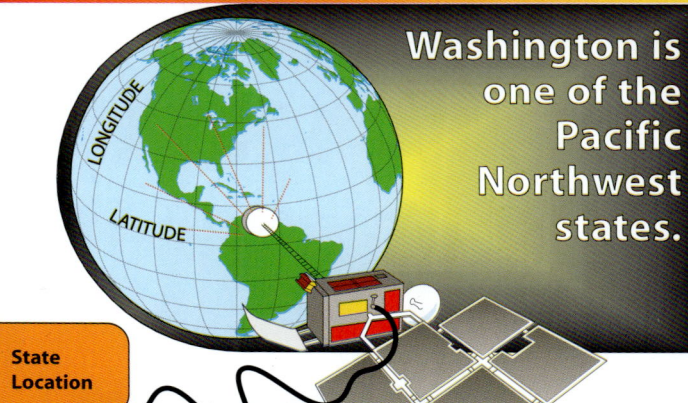

Washington is one of the Pacific Northwest states.

State Location

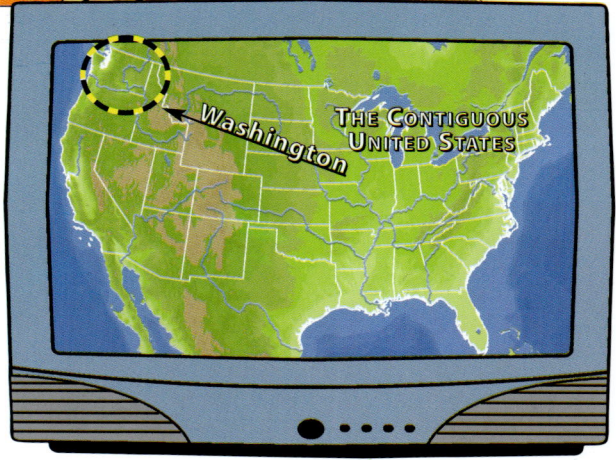

Word Definition

LATITUDE: Imaginary lines which run horizontally east and west around the globe
LONGITUDE: Imaginary lines which run vertically north and south around the globe

State Neighbors

On The Border!

These border Washington:

States:	Idaho Oregon
Country:	Canada
Bodies of water:	Pacific Ocean Columbia River Strait of Juan de Fuca Puget Sound Snake River

State Neighbors

East-West, North-South, Area

I'll Take the Low Road...

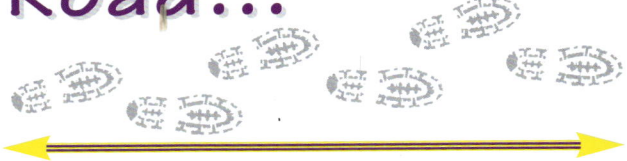

East-West, North-South, Area

Washington stretches 239 miles (385 kilometers) from north to south—or south to north. Either way, it's a long drive!

Total Area: Approximately 70,637 square miles (182,936 square kilometers)
Land Area: Approximately 66,581 square miles (172,431 square kilometers)

Washington is 370 miles (595 kilometers) from east to west—or west to east. Either way, it's *still* a long drive!

This is a compass rose. It helps you find the right direction on a map!

Highest & Lowest Points

You Take the High Road!

HIGHEST POINT
MOUNT RAINIER—14,410 FEET (4,392 METERS)

In 1792, England sent George Vancouver to the Puget Sound area. He mapped and named many land and sea features. He named Mount Rainier after a friend, Rear Admiral Peter Rainier.

LOWEST POINT
SEA LEVEL, AT THE PACIFIC OCEAN

State Counties

I'm County-ing on You!

Washington is divided into 39 counties.

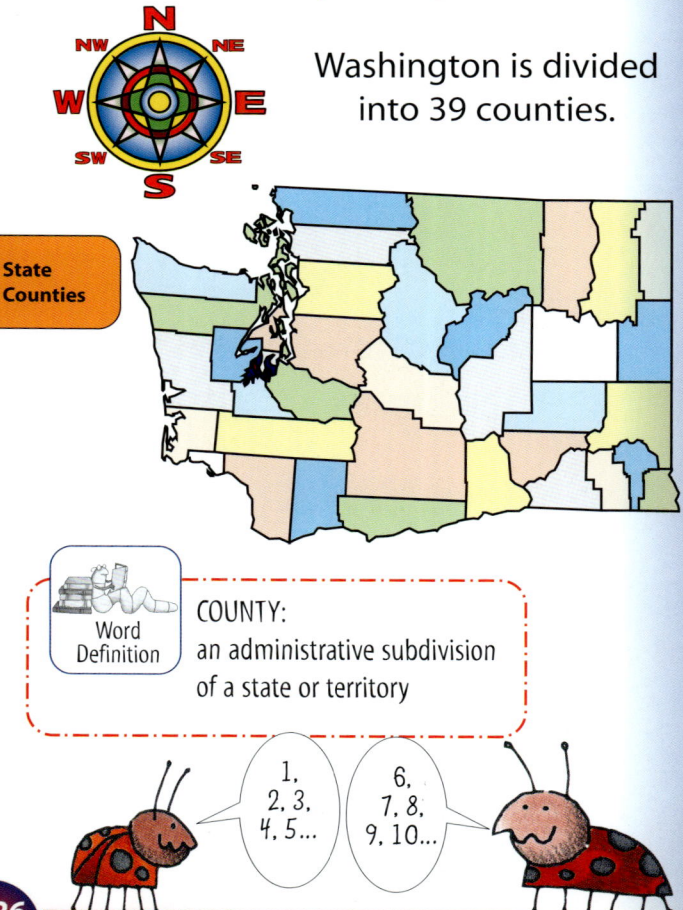

State Counties

Word Definition

COUNTY: an administrative subdivision of a state or territory

1, 2, 3, 4, 5...   6, 7, 8, 9, 10...

Natural Resources

It's All Natural!

Forests make up about 21.4 million acres (8.6 million hectares) in Washington.

Natural Resources

Word Definition

NATURAL RESOURCES: things that exist in or are formed by nature

Minerals and rocks:

- coal
- gold
- silver
- magnesium
- lead
- zinc
- limestone

Fish are another important natural resource in Washington.

Weather

Weather, Or Not?!

Washington's temperatures can drop to 21°F (-6°C) in the winter and reach 90°F (32°C) in the summer.

The Cascade Mountains divide Washington into two different weather regions. Western Washington has mild, wet winters and cool summers. Eastern Washington is drier, hotter in the summer, and colder in the winter.

Weather

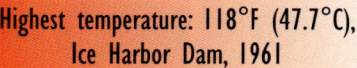

Highest temperature: 118°F (47.7°C), Ice Harbor Dam, 1961

°F=Degrees Fahrenheit °C=Degrees Celsius

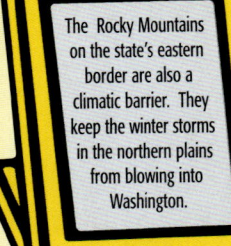

Lowest temperature: -48°F (-44.4°C), Mazama, 1968

The Rocky Mountains on the state's eastern border are also a climatic barrier. They keep the winter storms in the northern plains from blowing into Washington.

Topography

Back On Top

Washingtonians can walk along the Pacific Ocean in the morning and be at the top of Mount Rainier by noon. In just one day, Washingtonians can drive through their state and find beaches, dense forests, snow-covered mountains, rolling farmlands, and deserts. The Olympic Peninsula's topography ranges from sea level to the Olympic Mountains highland. The Puget Sound region has an irregular shoreline and includes more than 300 islands. Ranges of hills and low mountains dominate southwestern Washington. The Cascade Mountains are considered the "backbone" of the state and extend from Canada to the Columbia River. Much of the Columbia Plateau region is flat desert with ridges and rolling hills.

TOPOGRAPHY: the detailed mapping of the features of a small area or district

Word Definition

Topography

Sea Level
100 m / 328 ft
200 m / 656 ft
500 m / 1,640 ft
1,000 m / 3,281 ft
2,000 m / 6,562 ft
5,000 m / 16,404 ft

The "Inland Empire" is the part of Washington that lies east of the Cascade Mountains.

Mountains and Ranges

King of the Hill

- The **Cascade Mountains** are a recreation wonderland for hikers, mountain climbers, and skiers. The mountain range is dominated by five volcanoes—Glacier Peak, Mount Rainier, Mount Baker, Mount Adams, and Mount St. Helens which erupted in 1980.

- The rugged, snow-covered **Olympic Mountains** on the Olympic Peninsula are surrounded by evergreen rain forests. The tallest peak is Mount Olympus.

Mountains and Ranges

- The **Northern Rocky Mountains** are an extension of the Rocky Mountains and are found in Washington's northeastern corner. The tallest peaks in the Northern Rockies are Snow Peak and Copper Butte.

- The **Willapa Hills** are found in south Washington and are less than 3,000 feet (900 meters) in elevation.

- The **Blue Mountains** are located in the extreme southeastern area of the Columbia Plateau. The highest peak in the Blue Mountains is Rock Creek Butte.

Climb every mountain...

Rivers

Down The River

Here are some of Washington's major rivers:

- Cedar
- Chehalis
- Columbia
- Cowlitz
- Grays
- Lewis
- Nisqually
- Okanogan
- Pend Oreille
- Puyallup
- Sanpoil
- Skagit
- Snake
- Spokane
- Stillaguamish
- Willapa
- Yakima

Washington has some great rivers for white-water rafting and kayaking.

Grab a paddle!

Major Lakes

Gone Fishin'

Major Lakes

Major lakes in Washington include:

- Lake Franklin
- Lake Chelan
- Umatilla Lake
- Lake Wallula
- Potholes Reservoir
- Banks Lake
- Lake Washington
- Ross Lake
- Moses Lake
- Osoyoos Lake
- Lake Whatcom
- Swift Reservoir
- Merwin Lake
- Lake Cushman
- Yale Reservoir

Washington has more than 8,000 lakes and ponds. Lake Chelan is the largest natural lake. Lake Franklin is the largest reservoir.

Word Definition

RESERVOIR: a body of water stored for public use

Cities & Towns

ARE YOU A CITY MOUSE... OR A COUNTRY MOUSE?

The Outlook to Startup the Dusty Clipper is Plain.

Have you heard of these wonderful Washington town, city, or crossroad names? Perhaps you can start your own list!

Cities & Towns

UNIQUE NAMES:
- Cashmere
- Clipper
- Cotton
- Cougar
- Daisy
- Diamond
- Dusty
- Electric City
- Elk
- George
- Glacier
- Index
- Maiden
- Opportunity
- Outlook
- Plain
- Robe
- Startup

MAJOR CITIES:
- Seattle
- Spokane
- Tacoma
- Vancouver
- Bellevue

The Opportunity to find Cashmere, Cotton, and a Diamond is in the Index.

Transportation

Major Interstate Highways

I-5, I-82, I-90
There are 79,555 miles (128,028 kilometers) of roads and highways in Washington.

Railroads

More than 3,102 miles (4,992 kilometers) chug through Washington.

Transportation

Major Airports

Washington has an international airport between Seattle and Tacoma—the Seattle-Tacoma International Airport, commonly called Sea-Tac Airport.

Seaports

Lake Washington Ship Canal, Seattle, Tacoma, Vancouver, Longview, Kalama, Bellingham, Aberdeen/Hoquiam, Everett, Anacortes

Washington has a state ferry system which serves Puget Sound, the San Juan Islands, Vancouver Island, and the Olympic Peninsula.

Timeline

1592	Juan de Fuca sails along Washington's shores
1775	Bruno Heceta and Juan Francisco de la Bodega y Quadra are the first Europeans to see Washington
1792	Robert Gray sails into Grays Harbor and the Columbia River
1792	The coast of Washington and Puget Sound is surveyed by George Vancouver
1805	Lewis and Clark reach Washington and the Pacific Ocean
1810	British-Canadians establish fur trading post near present-day Spokane
1818	U.S. and Britain agree to joint occupation of Oregon region, including Washington
1846	Washington's boundary set at 49th parallel in a treaty between U.S. and Britain
1853	Congress creates Washington Territory
1855–1858	Indian Wars
1883	Northern Pacific Railroad links Washington and the East
1889	Washington becomes 42nd state
1909	Seattle hosts Alaska-Yukon-Pacific Exposition
1942	Grand Coulee Dam is completed
1962	World's Fair, Century 21, is held in Seattle
1964	U.S. and Canada give final approval to Columbia River Treaty of 1961
1974	World's Fair, Expo '74, is held in Spokane
1980	Mount St. Helen's erupts
1996	Gary Locke is elected first Chinese-American governor of a continental U.S. state

Early History

Here come the humans!

Early History

Thousands of years ago, ancient peoples inhabited Washington. They may have originally come across a frozen bridge of land between Asia and Alaska. If so, they slowly traveled east until some settled in what would one day become the state of Washington.

Archaeologists found a site near Palouse Falls that dates back about 10,000 years. They have found human bones, weapons, tools, elk remains, and bone needles at the dig.

These early people were nomadic hunters who traveled in small bands. They camped when seasons offered hunting, fishing, and fruit and nut gathering.

Early Indians

Native Americans Once Ruled!

The Cascade Mountains not only divided Washington geographically but also caused the development of two different Indian cultures.

West of the Cascades, the land is rich with natural resources. The rivers are full of fish, and the forests have lots of deer, elk, and other game. The major tribes to inhabit this area included the Chinook, Clallam, Clatsop, Makah, Nooksack, and Puyallup. They lived in red cedar longhouses.

East of the Cascades, the land has rolling hills and prairies. The Native Americans here moved often and lived in dugouts—shelters dug into the sides of hills and covered with grass mats. They fished, hunted wild game, and ate wild berries and roots. The major Indian tribes were the Cayuse, Colville, Nez Pérce, Spokane, and Yakima.

Though they lived on opposite sides of the Cascades, the Native Americans traded with each other. They developed a "trade language" to use when trading with people who spoke different languages.

Early Indians

Word Definition

WAMPUM: beads, pierced and strung, used by Indians as money or for ornaments

Exploration

Land Ho!

The search for a Northwest Passage (an inland water route which links the Atlantic and Pacific oceans) first brought Europeans to the Pacific Northwest. The Spanish and the English were the first to explore the northwest coast.

Exploration

In 1792, British Captain George Vancouver was the first European to finish a detailed survey of the Washington coast and the inland waterways. Vancouver joined the navy at the age of 13. He first sailed the Pacific Northwest coast with Captain James Cook in 1778. Vancouver mapped the Pacific Coast from San Luis Obispo, California, to Cook's Inlet, Alaska.

The United States, Great Britain, Spain, and Russia all laid claim to Oregon Country, the land that became the states of Washington and Oregon. Oregon came from an Indian name for the Columbia River.

George Vancouver named many Washington landmarks, including Mount Rainier, Mount Baker, and Puget Sound!

Settlement

Home, Sweet Home

John Jacob Astor, founder of the Pacific Fur Company, was the first American to establish a settlement in the Pacific Northwest. In 1811, his men built a trading post, Astoria (in present-day Oregon), at the mouth of the Columbia River. In 1812, the company also built forts at Okanogan (the first in present-day Washington) and Spokane.

Scotsman John McLoughlin of the British-owned Hudson's Bay Company built Fort Vancouver on the Columbia River in 1825. A few years later, the settlement had approximately 500 residents.

Settlement

After the fur traders, the next group to establish settlements was American missionaries and their wives. In 1836, Marcus and Narcissa Whitman journeyed from Missouri to the rolling hills near Walla Walla, Washington, to bring Christianity to the Indians. They established the first Christian mission among the Cayuse people.

In 1791, Spanish settlers founded the first European settlement in Washington on Neah Bay. The settlement was abandoned after five months.

Fur Trade

The fur trade was the hunting and trapping of animals for their furs. In Washington, beaver furs and seal furs were most important. The furs were valued because they were luxurious, durable, and water-repellent. The furs were used to make hats and clothing.

Fur traders took an interest in the Pacific Northwest after reading the reports of explorers Meriwether Lewis and William Clark. America's Pacific Fur Company, the Hudson's Bay Company of Great Britain, and the British-French Canadian North West Company competed with each other for furs.

Fur Trade

As the fur trading business grew, the companies established trading posts and settlements throughout Washington. Native Americans started working for the companies as hired trappers.

By the mid-1800s, furs had gone out of fashion, and the fur traders were turning to other businesses such as real estate, lumber, or railroads. Many continued to operate trading posts.

Legends and Lore

Sasquatch
(A.K.A. Bigfoot)

Sasquatch (Bigfoot) are large, hairy, human-like creatures thought to live in Washington's forests and mountains. Sasquatch weigh over 500 pounds (226.8 kilograms) and are 6–8 feet (1.8–2.4 meters) tall. Descriptions of Sasquatch report the creatures are covered with thick black hair, have a round human-like head, and smell like rotten meat. Footprints that have been found are shaped like a bear's foot and are more than 18 inches (45.7 centimeters) long. No one has ever found a dead Sasquatch or its skeleton remains.

Native Americans have told stories about the Sasquatch for hundreds of years. According to the stories Sasquatch look human but don't speak a human language. They sound more like animals. Other stories say they sing like an owl and charm people. The legends also say that sometimes Sasquatch enter camps, or houses, and steal food and children. What do you believe?

Legends and Lore

Revolution

Freedom!

Before Washington even became a territory, settlers in the 13 original colonies felt that England ignored their ideas and concerns.

In 1775, the colonies went to war with England. On July 4, 1776, the Declaration of Independence was signed.

While the colonists were fighting Great Britain, British explorer James Cook traveled to the Pacific Coast in search of a Northwest Passage. **Cook left Great Britain on July 12, 1776. He probably never knew the United States and Great Britain were at war!**

Revolution

James Cook also explored the Arctic Ocean before he died in 1779.

Slaves and Slavery

Early in U.S. history, Africans were brought to America to work on plantations. Thousands of slaves were brought to work on these large farms, growing and harvesting crops.

As settlers moved west, some took their slaves with them. Most of Washington's early settlers were fur traders and loggers. Some may have been slaveowners, but most were not.

Some of Washington's Native Americans owned slaves. When one tribe raided another, they would sometimes capture prisoners and force them to become their slaves. Slaves did the routine, heavy work. Slaves also hunted, fished, or made war alongside their masters. They could be sold, or traded, to other tribes.

Slaves and Slavery

Over time, some states abolished slavery, while others (many southern states) became more dependent on slavery. The fighting between the abolitionists and the slaveowners eventually led to the Civil War. In 1865, the 13th Amendment abolished slavery in the United

Word Definition

ABOLITIONIST: person who believed slavery was wrong and should be ended

The Civil War

Brother

The Civil War was fought between the American states. The argument was over states' rights to make their own decisions, including whether or not to own slaves. Some of the southern states began to secede (leave) the Union. They formed the Confederate States of America.

The fighting was a long way from Washington, so the territory continued to grow. In 1861, the University of Washington held its first classes. Walla Walla became the largest city in the territory after a gold strike in Idaho. Walla Walla became the supply point for the gold prospectors. Eastern Washington grew so much that part of it became the Idaho Territory when it was formed in 1863. During the Civil War, Washington residents also began to want statehood.

The Civil War

The Civil War

vs. Brother

The Civil War was also called the War Between the States. Soldiers often found themselves fighting against former friends and neighbors, even brother against brother. Those who did survive often went home without an arm, leg, or both, since amputation was the "cure" for most battlefield wounds. More Americans were killed during the Civil War than during World Wars I and II together!

The Civil War

In 1863, the Emancipation Proclamation, given by U.S. President Abraham Lincoln, freed the slaves still under Confederate control. Some slaves became sharecroppers; others went to Northern states to work in factories. Some went west—to Washington!

Famous Documents

Get It In Writing!

1776
Declaration of Independence

1789
U.S. Constitution

1846
U.S./Great Britain treaty sets boundary with Canada

1853
Washington Territory created

1889
State constitution approved

Immigrants

WELCOME TO AMERICA!

People have come to Washington from other states and many other countries on almost every continent! As time goes by, Washington's population grows more diverse. This means that people of different races and from different cultures and ethnic backgrounds have moved to Washington.

Immigrants

In the past, many immigrants have come to Washington from Europe and Asia. More recently, people have migrated to Washington from Hispanic countries such as Mexico. Only a certain number of immigrants are allowed to move to America each year. Many of these immigrants eventually become U.S. citizens.

Disasters & Catastrophes!

1829
Epidemics hit Indian tribes who have no resistance to diseases brought by Europeans and Americans.

1889
Fires destroy most of downtown Seattle and Spokane.

1902
The Yacolt Blaze burns more than 700,000 acres (283,290 hectares) of woodland between Bellingham, Washington, and Eugene, Oregon. Many people are killed and more than $13 million in property is destroyed or damaged.

Disasters & Catastrophes!

1910
Ninety-six people die when a Great Northern passenger train is buried by an avalanche near Wellington in Stevens Pass.

1962

Winds from Typhoon Frieda reach 160 miles (258 kilometers) per hour blowing roofs, smashing windows, uprooting trees and power poles, separating log booms, ripping an ocean liner loose from its moorings, and sinking a 10-car ferry at Lummi Island.

1980
Mount St. Helens erupts, killing 57 people and causing billions of dollars in damage.

2001
The strongest earthquake, centered about 35 miles (56 kilometers) from Seattle, to hit the Pacific Northwest in 52 years causes billions of dollars in damage.

Legal Stuff

1911
Workmen's compensation bill is approved

1912
State legislature approves a bill that gives direct power to voters to enact new laws or change existing laws

1917
Medical act sets up fund to help injured workers; both workers and employers contribute

Legal Stuff

1921
Washington establishes a Department of Health

1969
Washington establishes a court of appeals with 12 judges who are elected for six-year terms

Women & Children

1854

First territorial legislature provides for the establishment of common schools

1903, 1907

Child labor laws are approved by state legislature

Women & Children

1910

Women in Washington gain the right to vote

Wars

Fight! Fight! Fight!

Wars in which Washingtonians have participated:

- *War of 1812*
- *Mexican-American War*
- *Indian Wars*
- *The Pig War*
- *Civil War*
- *Spanish-American War*
- *World War I*
- *World War II*
- *Korean War*
- *Vietnam War*
- *Persian Gulf War*

Wars

Claim to Fame

An Apple a Day...

More apples are grown in Washington than in any other state in the U.S.!

Apples grow everywhere in Washington, both east and west of the Cascades Mountains. The best known apples are the Red Delicious and Gold Delicious, but more than 20 different varieties are grown in the state.

The first apple tree was planted in Washington in 1826 at Fort Vancouver. In 1854, the first orchard was begun near Oroville. By 1910, Washington was the nation's leading apple producer.

After planting, it takes two or three years before an apple tree bears fruit. A tree can produce apples for 20 to 30 years and can produce up to 20 boxes of apples each year. More than 12 billion apples are harvested each year from August through October. Between 35,000 and 45,000 workers pick each crop—by hand!

Washington celebrates its apples. Wenatchee's Washington State Apple Blossom Festival is the oldest major festival in the state.

The winner of the annual Washington State/University of Washington football game takes home the Apple Cup.

Indian Tribes

Cayuse
Chinook
Clatsop
Colville
Lummi
Makah
Nez Percé
Nisqually
Nooksack
Okanogan
Palouse

Puyallup
Quileute
Quinault
Samish
S'Klallam
Snohomish
Spokane
Walla Walla
Wenatchee
Yakima

Washington's coastal Indians held potlatches to show off their wealth. Potlatches were great feasts where the hosts gave nearly all they owned to their guests. *Wouldn't you like to be invited to that party!*

Indian Tribes

The greatest traders in the Pacific Northwest were the Chinook people. All the tribes used a trade language based on the Chinook language. The tribes met once a year at the Dalles, a fishing ground on the Columbia River, to trade goods, dance, and feast.

The Indians of Washington could not have known that the coming of the white man would mean an end to the way of life they had known for hundreds of years.

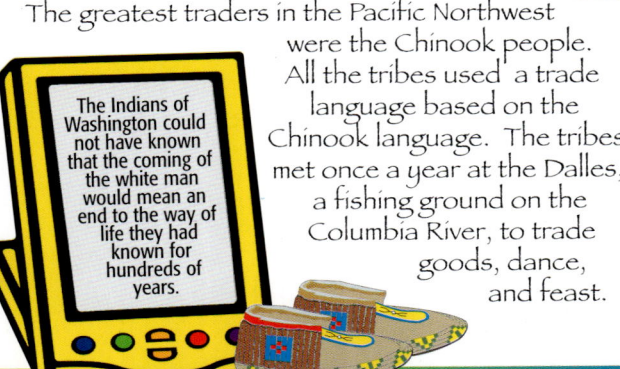

Explorers and Settlers

Here, There, Everywhere!

A Greek sea captain, **Apostolos Valerianos,** using the Spanish name Juan de Fuca, claimed he sailed Washington's coast and found a Northwest Passage in 1592.

In 1775, **Bruno Heceta and Juan de la Bodega y Quadra** claimed the land near present-day Point Grenville for Spain.

In 1778, **British explorer Captain James Cook** mapped the Washington Coast.

American **Captain Robert Gray** sailed to the Pacific Northwest in 1792. He explored the mouth of the Columbia River and named the river after his ship.

Explorers and Settlers

In 1805, **Meriwether Lewis and William Clark** traveled down the Columbia River and reached the Pacific Ocean 18 months after they left St. Louis, Missouri.

Bon Voyage!

State Founders

Founding Fathers

ARTHUR ARMSTRONG DENNY founded the settlement that became Seattle and wrote *Pioneer Days on Puget Sound*.

Scottish fur trader JOHN McLOUGHLIN founded the Hudson's Bay Company trading post at Fort Vancouver. He helped settlers and encouraged people to save and plant the seeds leftover from their meals.

MARCUS WHITMAN and his wife, NARCISSA, established several Indian missions in Washington Territory. He was killed by the Cayuse Indians who blamed the settlers for a measles epidemic.

Swedish immigrant NICHALAS DE LIN built the first water-driven sawmill in Tacoma in 1852.

Founding Mothers

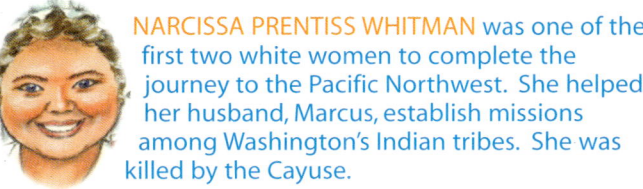

NARCISSA PRENTISS WHITMAN was one of the first two white women to complete the journey to the Pacific Northwest. She helped her husband, Marcus, establish missions among Washington's Indian tribes. She was killed by the Cayuse.

MOTHER JOSEPH led four Catholic nuns into Washington Territory in 1856 to build schools and hospitals for orphans, elderly, and the mentally ill.

Famous African-Americans

Former slave **GEORGE WASHINGTON** founded Centerville (now Centralia) in 1875. Washington traveled with his former owners, James and Hannah Cochran, to Washington Territory. He was denied free land because of his color, but the Cochrans staked a claim and then sold it to Washington. Later, Washington established Centerville and sold lots to families. It was one of the territory's most prosperous towns.

GEORGE BUSH was born a free man in Pennsylvania. He fought with Andrew Jackson at the Battle of New Orleans. He arrived in Oregon Territory in 1844, crossed the Columbia River into Washington and settled in an area called Bush Prairie. Bush and other pioneers helped keep Washington in the U.S. when the boundary between Canada and the U.S. was set at the 49th parallel.

Famous African-Americans

HORACE CAYTON owned a Seattle newspaper, *The Republic*. His wife, **SUSAN REVELS CAYTON**, was assistant editor and a writer. Her articles were also published in *The Seattle Post-Intelligencer*.

Ghosts

DID SOMEONE SAY BOO!?

Shorty is a ghost who haunts the Capitol Theater in Yakima. The theater is a live stage/movie theater, like many built across the U.S. before World War II. Shorty may have been a stagehand. No one is bothered by his presence. He doesn't like rock and roll music. Whenever a loud band is playing, lights go on and off and the sound system goes out. Backstage, there is a door located 12 feet off the floor. No stairs lead to it, and no one knows if there is a room behind the door. It's called Shorty's room, and the door is kept closed. Sometimes, the door is found swinging open!

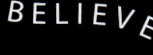

DO YOU BELIEVE IN GHOSTS?

Sports Stuff

EARL ANTHONY—bowler

DEBBIE ARMSTRONG—Olympic skier

EARL AVERILL—professional baseball player, named to Hall of Fame in 1975

JOANNE GUNDERSON CARNER—professional golfer

GRETCHEN FRASER—Olympic skier

KEN GRIFFEY, SR. AND KEN GRIFFEY, JR.—first father-son baseball players to play on the same team— the Seattle Mariners

STEVE LARGENT—record-setting professional football player

PHIL AND STEVE MAHRE—Olympic skiers

MEGAN QUANN—Olympic swimmer

RYNE SANDBURG—professional baseball player

TOM SNEVA—professional race car driver

Sports Stuff

> Fishing, hunting, and hiking are popular in the Evergreen State. Mountain climbing is a favorite, and the most challenging peak is 14,140-foot (4,392 meter) Mount Rainier.

Entertainers

BOB BARKER—television game show host

DYAN CANNON—actress

CAROL CHANNING—actress

KURT COBAIN—grunge musician

JUDY COLLINS—singer

BING CROSBY—singer

BOB CROSBY—musician

HOWARD DUFF—actor

FRANCES FARMER—actor

JIMI HENDRIX—rock and roll guitarist

GARY LARSON—cartoonist, creator of *The Far Side*

GYPSY ROSE LEE—entertainer

KENNY LOGGINS—singer, songwriter

KEVIN McCARTHY—actor

DARREN McGAVIN—actor

JOHN McINTIRE—actor

CRAIG T. NELSON—actor

JIMMIE RODGERS—singer

ADAM WEST—actor

MARTHA WRIGHT—singer

GIG YOUNG—actor

Authors

- **Mrs. Joseph Auslander (Audrey May Wurdemann)**—poet, won Pulitzer Prize for poetry

- **Frederick Faust**—author, wrote under 20 different pen names, including Max Brand and Evan Evans

- **Frank Herbert**—science fiction writer, author of Dune series

- **Mary McCarthy**—novelist known for her wit

- **Vernon Louis Parrington**—author, won the Pulitzer Prize for history

- **Theodore Roethke**—poet, taught at the University of Washington, won Pulitzer Prize and National Book Award

- **James G. Swan**—explorer, wrote an account of his experiences in the Puget Sound area

- **Theodore Winthrop**—explorer, wrote about his experiences living with Indians

Trivia: Who wrote a series of books about a warrior people who rode through the desert on giant worms?

Answer: Frank Herbert

Artists

GUY ANDERSON, KENNETH CALLAHAN, MORRIS GRAVES—painters, merged Asian painting techniques with colors found in the forest

SIR THOMAS BEECHAM—English conductor, directed the Seattle Symphony

DALE CHIHULY—sculptor, makes shell-like shapes out of glass

NELLIE CORNISH—pianist, opened the Cornish College of the Arts in Seattle

ROBERT JOFFREY—choreographer, founded Joffrey Ballet

JACOB LAWRENCE—artist whose work depicts African-American leaders such as Frederick Douglass and Harriet Tubman

CHARI MARKOWITZ—painter, sculptor; known for animal heads

Artists

PATRICE MUNSEL—singer, debuted at the Metropolitan Opera at age 17

GUSTAV SOHON—artist; drew the only surviving portraits of Indian chiefs in the Columbia River region

MARK TOBEY—artist, influenced by Asian art, developed style known as "white writing"

GEORGE TSUTAKAWA—sculptor, won acclaim for his fountains

Very Important People

DORSEY SYNG BAKER—banker and railroad executive; built railroad from Walla Walla to Wallula

WILLIAM EDWARD BOEING—engineer, industrialist; founded Boeing Airplane Company

WILLIAM O. DOUGLAS—judge, writer; served the longest term in history as a U.S. Supreme Court justice; wrote books about conservation

BILL GATES—computer programmer, developed first computer language for a personal computer; founded Microsoft Corporation with his partner, Paul Allen

JAMES JEROME HILL—industrialist, helped unite the Pacific Coast with the Great Lakes with the Great Northern Railway

ERIC A. JOHNSTON—businessman, served as president of the U.S. Chamber of Commerce and held government posts under several presidents

EDMUND R. MURROW—news reporter, considered "Father of Television News"

NORMAN RICE—first African-American mayor of Seattle

WILLIAM FRANCIS THOMPSON—conservationist

FREDERICK WEYERHAEUSER—lumber baron, built world's biggest sawmill in Everett

RUFUS WOODS—editor, publisher; campaigned to build the Grand Coulee Dam

Native Americans

SPOKAN GARRY—Spokane Indian chief and missionary, started schools and introduced Christianity to his people

CHIEF JOSEPH—Nez Percé chief; tried to lead his people to safety in Canada after being told to move from Oregon to Idaho; spent his last years on Colville reservation in Washington

KAMIAKIN—Yakima chief, led his people during Indian Wars of 1855

LESCHI—Nisqually chief, hanged for murders committed by his tribe during 1856 Seattle uprising

CHRISTINE QUINTASKET (HUMISHUMA OR MOURNING DOVE)—first Native American woman to write and publish a novel, *Cogewea, the Half-Blood: A Depiction of the Great Montana Cattle Range*

SEATHL (SEATTLE)—chief of Puget Sound area Indians, befriended early settlers; Seattle is named for him

SMOHALLA—medicine man and chief of the Wanapum, founded the Dreamer religious cult which encouraged Indians to return to traditional way of life and reject the settlers

SARAH WINNEMUCCA (THOCMETONY OR SHELL FLOWER)—spokeswoman for Indian rights

Native Americans

Political Leaders

BROCK ADAMS—U.S. representative, senator; secretary of transportation under President Jimmy Carter

RICHARD ACHILLES BALLINGER—mayor of Seattle, U.S. secretary of the interior under President William Taft

MARIA CANTWELL—U.S. senator, elected in 2000; served as state legislator and U.S. representative

JOHN EHRLICHMAN—advisor to President Richard Nixon; convicted of conspiracy and obstruction of justice in connection with Watergate scandal

DANIEL J. EVANS—governor, U.S. senator; backed Washington Wilderness bill and worked to improve trade with Pacific nations

ELISHA P. FERRY—first governor of Washington state

THOMAS FOLEY—U.S. representative, served as Speaker of the House

GARY LOCKE—Washington's first Chinese-American governor elected in 1996

SLADE GORTON—U.S. senator, championed environmental measures

HENRY MARTIN "SCOOP" JACKSON—U.S. representative and senator

WARREN G. MAGNUSON—U.S. senator

PATTY MURRAY—U.S. senator; elected in 1992 and 1998

DIXY LEE RAY—first woman governor of Washington

ISAAC STEVENS—first territorial governor of Washington

Good Guys, Patriots, & Bad Guy

FAY FULLER—first woman to climb Mount Rainier

SAM HILL—lawyer, businessman, and diplomat; designed and built the Peace Arch, the Stonehenge memorial to honor World War I soldiers, and the Maryhill Museum of Art

JOHN HUELSDONK—known as the "Iron Man of the Hoh;" tales of his strength and courage have made this logger a legend

HAZARD STEVENS—made the first recorded conquest of Mount Rainier

JONATHAN MAHEW WAINWRIGHT—U.S. Army general during World War II

JAMES W. WHITTAKER—first American to reach the summit of Mount Everest

BAD GUY:

A hijacker identified as **D.B. COOPER** on the passenger list boarded a Northwest Airlines flight in Seattle on November 24, 1971. He demanded and was paid $200,000. He took the money and parachuted from the plane somewhere over the southern Cascades. He hasn't been seen since, but school children did find some of the money on the banks of the Columbia River.

Good Guys, Patriots, & Bad Guy

Churches and Schools

Keeping the Faith

Claquato Church, Chehalis—oldest church in the state, built in 1858

Cathedral of St. John the Evangelist, Spokane—fine example of Gothic church architecture

Log Church, Chelan—dates back to 1898

Saint James Cathedral, Seattle—Neo-Baroque church built in 1907

Saint Peter's Episcopal Church, Tacoma—Gothic Revival church

Trinity Episcopal Church, Seattle—built in 1891 to resemble an English country parish church

SCHOOLS

Central Washington University, Ellensburg

Evergreen State College, Olympia

Pacific Lutheran University, Tacoma

University of Washington, Seattle

Washington State University, Pullman

Whitman College, Walla Walla

The University of Washington was the first territorial university in the Pacific Northwest.

Historic Sites and Parks

HISTORIC SITES

EBY'S LANDING NATIONAL HISTORICAL RESERVE, WHIDBEY ISLAND—settlement founded in the 1850s

KLONDIKE GOLD RUSH NATIONAL HISTORICAL PARK, SEATTLE—southern unit of a park located in Skagway, Alaska, which honors Seattle's role in the Gold Rush

MONTICELLO CONVENTION SITE, LONGVIEW—location where Washington residents petitioned the federal government to separate Washington from Oregon

NEZ PERCÉ NATIONAL HISTORIC PARK, COLVILLE INDIAN RESERVATION—Two of 38 sites that commemorate Nez Percé culture and history are located on the Colville Indian Reservation near Spokane. Other sites are located in Idaho, Oregon, and Montana

PIONEER SQUARE HISTORIC DISTRICT, SEATTLE—city's oldest neighborhood, an 18-block area of restored buildings

PORT GAMBLE—milltown built in 1863

SAN JUAN ISLAND NATIONAL HISTORIC PARK—honors the bloodless dispute that occurred when both the U.S. and Great Britain claimed San Juan Island

TILLICUM VILLAGE, BLAKE ISLAND—Indian longhouse

WHITMAN MISSION NATIONAL HISTORICAL SITE, NEAR WALLA WALLA—honors the Indian mission founded by Marcus and Narcissa Whitman in 1836

Historic Sites and Parks

Home, Sweet Home!

BIGELOW HOUSE, OLYMPIA—built in 1854 for Judge Daniel Bigelow, it has been continuously occupied since it was built

CAMPBELL HOUSE, SPOKANE—built in 1898 by Amasa B. Campbell, who made his fortune from mining

HOQUIAM'S CASTLE, HOQUIAM—mansion built by lumber tycoon Robert Lytle

H.M. GILBERT HOMEPLACE, YAKIMA—built in 1898 by pioneer in irrigation

EZRA MEEKER MANSION, PUYALLUP—restored 17-room house built in 1889

PERKINS HOUSE, COLFAX—built by Colfax founder James Perkins between 1884 and 1886

GEORGE E. PICKETT HOUSE, BELLINGHAM—built in 1856 for Pickett, who later led the Confederate charge at the Battle of Gettysburg

PIONEER FARM MUSEUM, NORTH OF EATONVILLE—replica of 1880s farm

STIMSON-GREEN MANSION, SEATTLE—Kirtland Cutter designed this house in 1899

Forts

A few of Washington's famous Forts

FORT BORST, CENTRALIA—built in the 1850s to protect settlers from Indians

FORT COLUMBIA, CHINOOK—built in 1895 to protect the coast

FORT LEWIS, TACOMA—established in 1917, home of I Corps

FORT NISQUALLY, DUPONT—reconstruction of post built in 1833 by Hudson's Bay Company

FORT SIMCOE, NEAR WHITE SWAN—built in 1856 during the Yakima War

FORT SPOKANE, NEAR GRAND COULEE DAM—Army outpost built in 1880 to keep peace between Indians and settlers

FORT STEILACOOM, STEILACOOM—built in 1849 to protect settlers from Indians

FORT VANCOUVER, VANCOUVER—reconstruction of western headquarters of Hudson's Bay Company

FORT WARD, BAINBRIDGE ISLAND—built in 1910 to protect Bremerton's navy yard

Forts

Libraries

Check out the following special Washington libraries! (Do you have a library card? Have you worn it out yet?!)

STATE LAW LIBRARY, Olympia

UNIVERSITY OF WASHINGTON, SEATTLE— largest collection of Pacific Northwest history in the country

NORTH CENTRAL REGIONAL LIBRARY, Wenatchee

SEATTLE PUBLIC LIBRARY

WASHINGTON STATE UNIVERSITY LIBRARY, Pullman

WASHINGTON STATE LIBRARY, OLYMPIA— Washington's first library opened in 1853 to serve legislators and government officials

Libraries

Washington's first public library opened in 1858 in Steilacoom.

Zoos and Attractions

CAT TALES ENDANGERED SPECIES CONSERVATION PARK, MEAD—home to more than two dozen big cats
HELLS CANYON, ON THE SNAKE RIVER IN SOUTHEASTERN WASHINGTON—deepest canyon in North America
HOLLAND GARDENS, OAK HARBOR—gardens surrounding a windmill
OLYMPIC GAME FARM, SEQUIM—home to exotic animals that have retired from show business
PEACE ARCH STATE PARK, BLAINE—six-story arch on the U.S.-Canadian border which commemorates the countries' friendship
POINT DEFIANCE ZOO AND AQUARIUM, TACOMA—home to polar bears, otters, walruses, and sea life
SEATTLE AQUARIUM—underwater view of Puget Sound sea life
SPACE NEEDLE, SEATTLE—a 607-foot (185-meter) observation tower built for the 1962 World's Fair
WRIGHT PARK ARBORETUM, TACOMA—exotic trees, shrubs, and statuary
WOLF HAVEN INTERNATIONAL, TENINO—home to two dozen gray wolves
WOODLAND PARK ZOO, SEATTLE—outstanding natural attractions

Zoos and Attractions

Museums

- State Capitol Museum, Olympia
- Museum of History, Seattle
- Museum of Native American Cultures, Spokane
- Cheney Cowles Museum, Spokane
- Lewis County Historical Museum, Chehalis
- Adam East Museum, Moses Lake
- Thomas Burke Memorial Museum, Seattle
- Suquamish Museum, Suquamish
- Pacific Science Center, Seattle
- Hanford Science Center, Richland
- Bremerton Naval Museum
- Museum of Flight, Seattle
- Whale Museum, Friday Harbor
- Wing Luke Asian Museum, Seattle
- Museum of Native American Cultures, Spokane
- Naval Shipyard Museum, Bremerton
- Maryhill Museum of Art, Goldendale
- Makah Cultural and Research Center, Neah Bay

Museums

Monuments and Memorials

Lest We Forget

MONUMENTS

MOUNT ST. HELENS NATIONAL VOLCANIC MONUMENT, near Castle Rock

STONEHENGE, MARYHILL— memorial to soldiers who died in World War I

MEMORIALS

GRAVE OF CHIEF SEATTLE, Suquamish
CHIEF JOSEPH MEMORIAL, Colville Reservation
STEPTOE BATTLEFIELD MEMORIAL, Rosalia
VOLUNTEER PARK, Seattle

The Arts

SEATTLE CENTER OPERA HOUSE is home to Seattle Symphony Orchestra, Seattle Youth Symphony, and the Seattle Opera Association

SEATTLE CHILDREN'S THEATER presents a variety of drama and entertainment for children at the **CHARLOTTE MARTIN THEATER** in Seattle Center.

CORNISH COLLEGE OF THE ARTS offers programs in music and other arts in Seattle

THE TACOMA DOME AND PANTAGES THEATER host actors, dancers, and comedians.

COLUMBIA ARTS CENTER in Vancouver has a continuing schedule of live theater, music, and dance.

The Arts

MOUNT BAKER THEATER in Bellingham features crystal chandeliers and a Wurlitzer 210-pipe organ.

To be, or not to be involved in the arts, that is the question. What is your answer?

Seashores & Lighthouses

Seashores

Washington has 157 miles (253 kilometers) of coastline. If you include the outer coast, bays, rivers, creeks, and offshore islands, Washington has about 3,026 miles (4,870 kilometers) of coastline.

The San Juan Islands are an archipelago (a group or chain of islands) of 172 islands. The islands were shared by the Americans and the British until 1872 when Kaiser Wilhelm I of Germany awarded the islands to the U.S.

Let There Be Light!

Cape Disappointment Lighthouse, Ilwaco— built in 1856, oldest in the Pacific Northwest.
Destruction Island Lighthouse, Ruby Beach
Cape Flattery Lighthouse, Tatoosh Island
Mukilteo Lighthouse, Mukilteo
Admiralty Head Lighthouse, Whidbey Island
Browns Point Lighthouse, Tacoma
Alki Point Lighthouse, Seattle

Roads and Bridges

Roads

Mount Baker Scenic Byway begins in Glacier and ends in Artist Point. Artist Point is closed in the winter.

North Cascades Highway winds from Sedro Woolley to Winthrop on Washington 20.

Sherman Pass Scenic Byway travels from Republic to Franklin Roosevelt Lake.

Spirit Lake Memorial Highway is at Mount St. Helens.

Washington 109, U.S. 101, the Moclips Highway, and the **Dungeness Scenic Loop** takes travelers on a tour of the Olympic Peninsula.

Bridges

Four of the world's eight floating bridges are in Washington—the side-by-side bridges on I-90 (the **Albert D. Rossellini Bridge**) and the **Hood Canal Bridge.**

Bridge design award winners include the **Cicero Bridge** on the north fork of the Stillguamish River, the **Cowlitz River Bridge** near Mossyrock, and the **Selah Creek** twin bridges near Yakima.

The **Astoria-Megler Bridge**, the longest continuous steel span truss bridge in the world, crosses the mouth of the Columbia River and connects Washington to Oregon.

Caves

LAVA TUBE CAVES

Washington is home to many lava tube caves, which are found only in the western states. Lava tube caves form when flowing basalt lava cools rapidly enough to solidify on the top and bottom, but molten lava keeps flowing through the cooling crust.

APE CAVE, on the south side of Mount St. Helens, is the longest, unbroken lava tube cave in the Western Hemisphere.

ICE CAVE, Big Four Mountain, formed in massive fields of ice caused by avalanches.

GARDNER CAVE, Crawford State Park, is a limestone cavern.

LAKE CAVE, OLE'S CAVE, and CHEESE CAVE are all part of the Mount Baker-Mount St. Helens lava flows.

- **WHICH IS THE STALAGMITE?**
- **WHICH IS THE STALACTITE?**

Caves

Answer: Stalactites are long, tapering formations hanging from the roof of a cavern, produced by continuous watery deposits containing certain minerals. The mineral-rich water dripping from stalactites often forms conical stalagmites on the floor below.

Word Definition

SPELUNKER: a person who goes exploring caves for fun

Animals

Washington's Animals include:

- Bear
- Deer
- Beaver
- Marten
- Mink
- Muskrat
- Bobcat
- Gopher
- Mountain Lion
- Mountain Goat
- Badger
- Marmot
- Flying Squirrel
- Elk

Herds of Roosevelt, or Olympic, elk, the largest members of the deer family, can be found on the Olympic Peninsula.

Wildlife Watch

Some endangered Washington animals are:

Black Right Whale
Blue Whale
Brown Pelican
Columbian White-tailed deer
Fin Whale
Gray Wolf
Leatherback Sea Turtle
Peregrine Falcon
Sei Whale
Sperm Whale
Woodland Caribou

Federal law lists 13 animals and six plants that are endangered or threatened in Washington. State law lists another 35 animals that are endangered or threatened.

Wildlife Watch

Birds

You may spy these birds in Washington:

- Pheasant
- Quail
- Ruffed Grouse
- Western Lark
- Sage Grouse
- Duck
- Goose
- Owl
- Hawk
- Goldfinch
- Bald Eagle
- Golden Eagle
- Pelican
- Oystercatcher
- Turkey Vulture
- Waxwing
- Falcon

A hummingbird's wings beat 75 times a second—so fast that you only see a blur! They make short squeaky sounds, but do not sing.

Insects

Don't let these Washington bugs bug you!

- Mayfly
- Dragonfly
- Grasshopper
- Cricket
- Giant Water Bug
- Water Strider
- Assassin Bug
- Spittlebug
- Ground Beetle
- Ladybug Beetle
- Monarch Butterfly
- Sphinx Moth
- Crane Fly
- Mosquito
- Honeybee
- Bumblebee
- Ant

Bumblebee

Ants

Mosquito

Monarch Butterfly

Ladybug

Grasshopper

Do we know any of these bugs?

Maybe... Hey, that ladybug is cute!

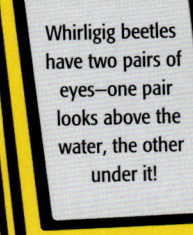

Whirligig beetles have two pairs of eyes—one pair looks above the water, the other under it!

Insects

Fish

- **Rainbow Trout**
- **Cutthroat Trout**
- **Steelhead Trout**
- **Whitefish**
- **Sturgeon**
- **Cod**
- **Salmon**
- **Flounder**
- **Halibut**
- **Albacore Tuna**

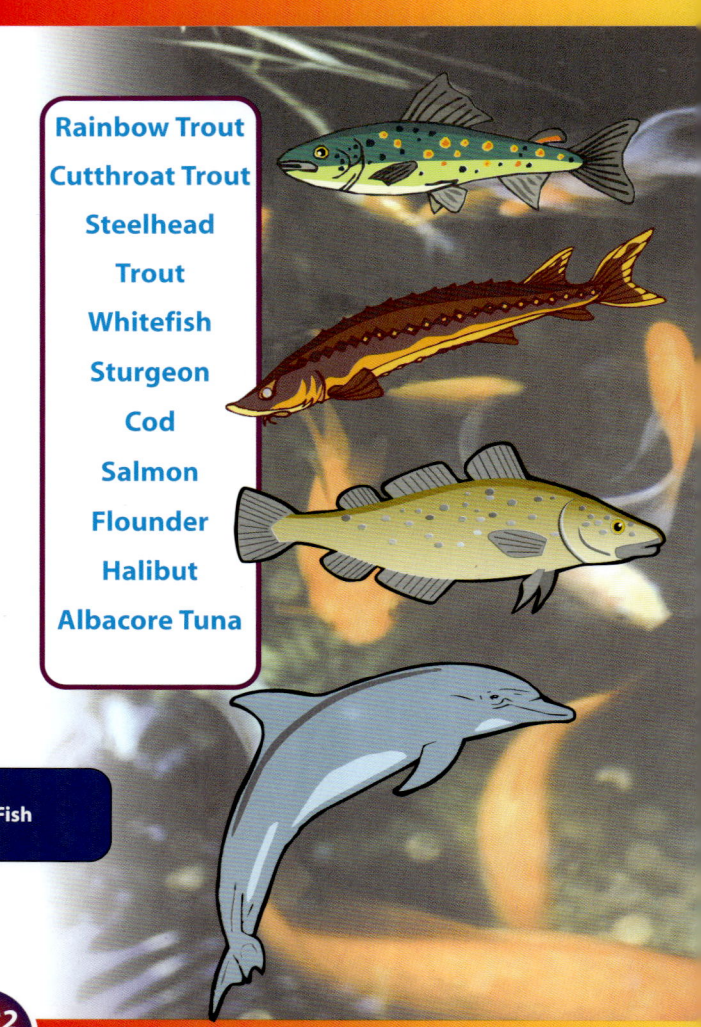

Fish

Sea Critters

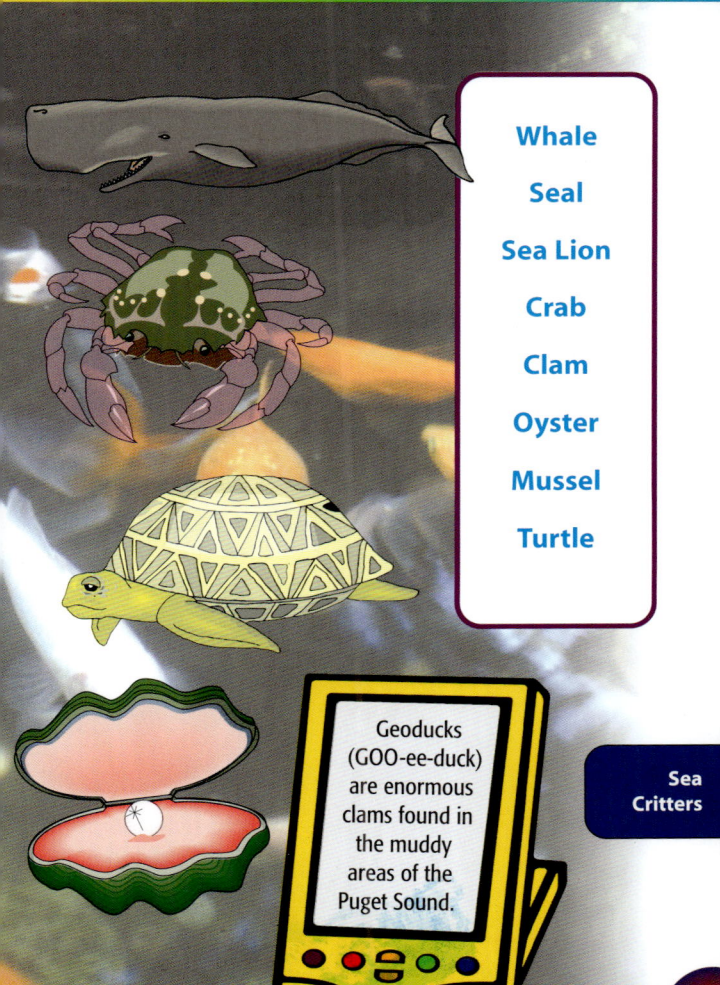

- Whale
- Seal
- Sea Lion
- Crab
- Clam
- Oyster
- Mussel
- Turtle

Geoducks (GOO-ee-duck) are enormous clams found in the muddy areas of the Puget Sound.

Sea Critters

Seashells

She sells seashells by the Washington seashore!

- Limpet
- Abalone
- Nerite
- Cerith
- Periwinkle
- Slipper Shell
- Moon Snail
- Murex
- Olive Shell
- Cockle
- Shipworm
- Tusk Shell

Seashells

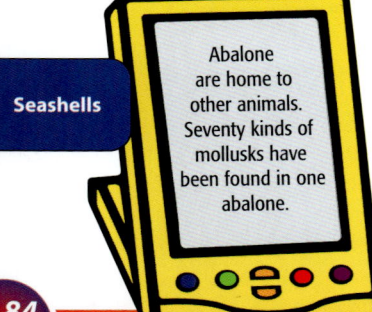

Abalone are home to other animals. Seventy kinds of mollusks have been found in one abalone.

Rock and Roll!

Trees

TREEMENDOUS!

These trees tower over Washington:

- DOUGLAS FIR
- PONDEROSA PINE
- SITKA SPRUCE
- WESTERN HEMLOCK
- WESTERN RED CEDAR
- WESTERN LARCH
- LODGEPOLE PINE
- ALDER
- ASH
- ASPEN
- COTTONWOOD
- MAPLE

Wildflowers

Are you crazy about these Washington flowers?

- Brown-eyed Susan
- Goldenrod
- Lupine
- Western Rhododendron
- Monkey Flower
- Mountain Phlox
- Heather
- Queen Anne's Lace
- Flett's Violet
- Sunflower
- Everlasting Lily
- Fireweed

Flower Power!

Wildflowers

Cream of the Crops

Agricultural products from Washington:

Wheat

Potatoes

Pears

Apples

Barley

Apricots

Cherries

Sugar Beets

Grapes

Plums

Flower bulbs

Hay

Cream of the Crops

Asparagus

Oats

Rye

First/Big/Small/Etc.

The oldest operating gas station in the U.S. is in Zillah.

The first Father's Day was held June 19, 1910, in Spokane. It was the idea of Sonora Louise Smart Dodd, whose father raised his six children alone after his wife died.

Washington's state capitol building was the last one built with a rotunda.

Cape Flattery on the Olympic Peninsula is the most northwestern point in the contiguous U.S.

The world's first soft-serve ice cream machine was located in a Dairy Queen in Olympia.

The smallest city to host a World's Fair was Spokane in 1974.

During the winter of 1998–99, Mount Baker had the most snow ever recorded in one place in one year—1,124 inches (2,855 centimeters).

The world's first non-stop flight across the Pacific Ocean ended at East Wenatchee's Fancher Field on October 5, 1931. It started in Toyko, Japan, and took 41 hours, 13 minutes.

The Grand Coulee Dam on the Columbia River in north central Washington is one of the world's largest hydroelectric facilities, one of the largest concrete dams in the world, and is home to the world's largest laser light show.

Festivals

Celebrate!

Great Bavarian Ice Fest, Leavenworth—January
Skagit Valley Tulip Festival, Mount Vernon—March–April
Ellensburg Rodeo, Ellensburg—September
Seattle International Children's Festival—May
Langley's Mystery Weekend, Langley—February
Bumbershoot, Seattle—September
Walla Walla Sweet Onion Festival, Walla Walla—July
Sea to Ski Festival, Bellingham—May
Washington State Apple Blossom Festival, Wenatchee—April
Shoalwater Bay Nation PowWow, Westport—April
Chief Seattle Days, Suquamish—August
Spokane Indian Days Encampment/PowWow, Spokane Reservation—August
Cherry Blossom and Japanese Cultural Festival, Seattle—April
Festival Sundiata, Seattle—February
Northwest Folklife Festival, Seattle—May

Holidays

Calendar

Martin Luther King, Jr. Day, *3rd Monday in January*	Groundhog Day *February 2*	Presidents' Day, *3rd Monday in February*
Memorial Day, *last Monday in May*	Independence Day, *July 4*	Labor Day, *1st Monday in September*
Columbus Day, *2nd Monday in Ocotober*	Veterans Day, *November 11*	Thanksgiving, *4th Thursday in November*

Christmas, Chanukah, Kwanzaa, Vietnamese Tet, and Chinese New Year are all special celebrations in Washington.

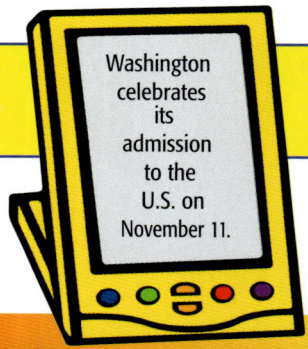

Washington celebrates its admission to the U.S. on November 11.

Holidays

Famous Food

Washington is famous for the following foods!

- Salmon Steaks
- Apple Pie
- Cherry Tarts
- Walla Walla Sweet Onions
- Pear Preserves
- Willapa Bay oysters
- Wild Blackberries
- Sturgeon Filets
- Pan-fried Trout
- Coffee

Yum, yum. This is great! Let's dig in!

Business & Trade

WASHINGTON WORKS!

Washington has a diverse economy with several major industries including manufacturing, agriculture, and trade.

Manufacturers in Washington build airplanes, boats, trucks, and equipment for space exploration. They also make lumber and plywood, process and package food, and generate electricity.

Forest products were Washington's first major industry. Washington ranks among the leading states in lumber and wood products, including wood pulp, paper, plywood, shingles, and shakes.

Washington is a leader in the development of waterpower resources and the production of hydroelectricity. Dams that harness Washington's rivers also provide irrigation water for eastern Washington's agriculture. Wheat, apples, and flower bulbs are among the state's leading crops.

Seattle is the gateway to the Pacific Rim. Air and sea transport to Alaska, Hawaii, and Asia is a major industry. Chief ports are Seattle, Tacoma, Anacortes, Bellingham, Everett, Longview, Vancouver, and Grays Harbor.

> Seattle and Spokane are chief hubs for rail transportation. Two transcontinental lines cross Washington.

Books & Websites

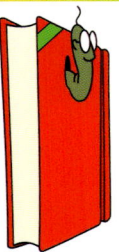

My First Book About Washington by Carole Marsh

Kids Learn America by Patricia Gordon and Reed C. Snow

Let's Discover the States: Washington by the Aylesworths

The Washington Experience Series by Carole Marsh

Cool Washington Websites

http://www.state.wa.us

http://www.washingtonexperience.com

http://www.50states.com

http://www.netstate.com

Washington Glossary

GLOSSARY WORDS

constitution—a document outlining the role of a government

emancipation—to be set free

hydroelectric—generated by water power

revolution—the overthrow of a government

secede—to voluntarily give up being part of an organized group

sound—a broad channel between two large bodies of water, or between an island and the mainland

strait—a narrow body of water that joins two larger bodies

territory—an area of a country that is not a state, but has a separate, organized government

Spelling List

Washington Spelling Bee

Here are some special Washington-related words to learn! To take the Spelling Bee, have someone call out the words and you spell them aloud or write them on a piece of paper.

SPELLING WORDS

- Cascades
- Chinook
- Columbia
- evergreen
- glacier
- hemlock
- lumber
- mountain
- northwest
- Olympia
- Pacific
- potlatch
- Rainier
- rhododendron
- salmon
- Sasquatch
- Spokane
- transcontinental
- volcano
- Washington
- Wenatchee

About the Author

ABOUT THE AUTHOR...

CAROLE MARSH has been writing about Washington for more than 20 years. She is the author of the popular Washington State Stuff Series for young readers and creator along with her son, Michael Marsh, of Washington Facts and Factivities, a CD-ROM widely used in Washington schools. The author of more than 100 Washington books and other supplementary educational materials on the state, Marsh is currently working on a new collection of Washington materials for young people. Marsh correlates her Washington materials to the Washington learning standards. Many of her books and other materials have been inspired by or requested by Washington teachers and librarians.

EDITORIAL ASSISTANT:
Pam Dufresne

GRAPHIC DESIGNER:
Victoria DeJoy